T0196032

BILINGUAL MEDITATIONS – MEDITACIONES BILINGÜES

Improving Yourself and Your Spanish at the Same Time

—— YVETTE CITIZEN ——

BALBOA.PRESS
A DIVISION OF HAY HOUSE

Copyright © 2020 Yvette Citizen.

All rights reserved. No part of this book may be used or reproduced by any means, graphic, electronic, or mechanical, including photocopying, recording, taping or by any information storage retrieval system without the written permission of the author except in the case of brief quotations embodied in critical articles and reviews.

Balboa Press books may be ordered through booksellers or by contacting:

Balboa Press
A Division of Hay House
1663 Liberty Drive
Bloomington, IN 47403
www.balboapress.com
844-682-1282

Because of the dynamic nature of the Internet, any web addresses or links contained in this book may have changed since publication and may no longer be valid. The views expressed in this work are solely those of the author and do not necessarily reflect the views of the publisher, and the publisher hereby disclaims any responsibility for them.

The author of this book does not dispense medical advice or prescribe the use of any technique as a form of treatment for physical, emotional, or medical problems without the advice of a physician, either directly or indirectly. The intent of the author is only to offer information of a general nature to help you in your quest for emotional and spiritual well-being. In the event you use any of the information in this book for yourself, which is your constitutional right, the author and the publisher assume no responsibility for your actions.

Any people depicted in stock imagery provided by Getty Images are models, and such images are being used for illustrative purposes only. Certain stock imagery © Getty Images.

The Spanish sections of this book were edited by Renata Yawn, Federally Certified Court Interpreter.

Print information available on the last page.

ISBN: 978-1-9822-5304-2 (sc)
ISBN: 978-1-9822-5305-9 (e)

Library of Congress Control Number: 2020915291

Balboa Press rev. date: 09/11/2020

Dedicated to all my bilingual brothers and sisters out there who are breaking barriers and uniting worlds.

Dedicado a todas mis hermanas y hermanos bilingües que están rompiendo barreras y uniendo mundos.

Also dedicated to my best friend and love of my life, my husband, Juan, and to my siblings, Angela and Pedro, whose joyful spirits always uplift me.

También dedicado a mi mejor amigo y el amor de mi vida, mi esposo, Juan, y mis hermanos, Ángela y Pedro, cuyos espíritus alegres siempre me animan.

And in memory of my parents, Gene and Beatriz, and of Erik and David. You are always in my heart.

Y en memoria de mis padres, Eugenio y Beatriz, y de Erik y de David. Los llevo siempre en mi corazón.

Contents

Tips for Using This Book

The goal of this book is to help you improve your life and your Spanish at the same time. It is geared for people with at least a basic knowledge of Spanish who want to revive or extend their Spanish language skills and are interested in self-improvement. This way, one can simultaneously work on both practices without having to set aside specific times for each.

This book consists of meditative exercises designed to help you get into a more positive frame of mind while improving your Spanish language skills. The book is divided into ten sections. Each one consists of a meditative exercise with instructions in Spanish followed by an English translation. There is a Spanish-English glossary of selected terms at the end of each section for you to consult and review frequently to reinforce your Spanish vocabulary. Blank glossary pages are included in each section for you to add new terminology.

There are many ways to use this book; you should choose the method that best works for you. One suggestion is to first read a passage in Spanish and see how much you understand. Then read the English translation of the passage to see if you misunderstood anything. Try doing the recommended exercises in Spanish if you can. Or do them in English and then translate them into Spanish. You can do these exercises alone, with a partner, or with your Sunday morning Spanish club. The exercises can be done before or after a formal traditional meditation session or be used as a positive and instructional way to start or end the day. You decide.

You should always have a bilingual dictionary handy. I recommend www.wordreference.com and the *Oxford Spanish/ English Dictionary*. Both have apps you can download to your smartphone, but there are many other resources as well.

Have fun! ¡Diviértete!

If you would like to receive free audio recordings in English and Spanish of Chapters 1 & 2 of this book, please contact Yvette, the author, through her website, www. TheConfidentInterpreter.com.

A Word About Glossaries

The premade and blank glossaries have been added to encourage and facilitate your vocabulary acquisition. Use them to write down terms you had to look up or you found interesting. You can also create a more general and personalized glossary on a computer file or an old-fashioned notebook; the trick is to make your glossary an active and accessible document that you look at often. Make it fun! Draw in it, add emojis, images, stickers, photos, and anything else that will encourage you to visit it repeatedly and keep it alive. You can also make audio recordings of your glossary terms and listen to them at your convenience.

Sueños y Visiones

Toda gran obra empieza con un sueño o una visión. Piensa en algo que has soñado ser, hacer o tener. Imagina los detalles que forman parte de tu sueño. Ahora, imagínate a ti mismo viviendo ese sueño. Visualiza todos los detalles que puedas. Por ejemplo, si tu sueño es vivir en la casa ideal para ti, imagina que ya estás viviendo allí. ¿Qué se siente estar en esa casa? ¿Cómo es tu cocina ideal? ¿Qué tal la recámara? ¿El patio? ¿La sala?

Si tu sueño tiene que ver con el trabajo perfecto, imagínalo con el mayor detalle posible. ¿Cuáles son tus deberes? ¿Cómo es tu lugar de trabajo? ¿Tienes tu propia oficina? ¿Cómo son tus colegas? ¿Requiere que viajes?

Ejercicio

Sea cual sea tu sueño, dilo en voz alta en español o, mejor aún, anótalo en un cuaderno o en tu computadora. Si es necesario, puedes escribirlo en inglés primero y luego traducirlo al español. Busca los términos que no te sepas y agrégalos a tu glosario. Al hacerlo, intensificarás tu intención de lograrlo porque lo podrás visualizar mejor y también aumentarás tu vocabulario en español.

Repite a menudo a este ejercicio. Explora diferentes sueños. Así, tu mente se concentrará en tus metas y extenderás tu vocabulario al mismo tiempo.

1

Dreams and Visions

All great works begin with a dream or a vision. Think of something you have dreamed of doing, having, or being. Imagine the details that form part of your dream. Now imagine yourself as if you were living your dream. Visualize as many details as you can. For example, if your dream is to live in your ideal house, imagine that you're already living there. What does it feel like to be in that house? What is your ideal kitchen like? What about the bedroom? The yard? The living room?

If your dream is about having the perfect job, imagine it with as much detail as possible. What are your duties? What is your workplace like? Do you have your own office? What are your colleagues like? Does it require travel?

Exercise

Whatever your dream may be, say it out loud in Spanish, or even better, write it down in your notebook or on your computer. If you need to, you can write it in English first and then translate it into Spanish. Look up the terms you don't know and add them to your glossary. In doing so, you will intensify your intention to achieve it because you will visualize it better and you'll be increasing your Spanish vocabulary.

Come back to this exercise frequently. Explore different dreams. You will focus your mind on your goals and expand your Spanish vocabulary at the same time.

Glosario: Sueños y Visiones
Glossary: Dreams and Visions

1.	obra	work (as in work of art or great works)
2.	empieza	begins
3.	soñado	dreamed
4.	ser, hacer o tener	be, do, or have
5.	cocina	kitchen
6.	recámara	bedroom
7.	sala	living room
8.	mayor detalle posible	as much detail as possible
9.	deberes	duties, responsibilities
10.	lugar de trabajo	workplace
11.	oficina	office
12.	colegas	colleagues
13.	sca cual sea	whatever it may be
14.	cuaderno	notebook
15.	busca	look up, look for, search
16.	sepas (del verbo 'saber') (que no te sepas)	know (that you don't know)
17.	agrégalos	add them to
18.	intensificarás	you will intensify
19.	visualizar	visualize
20.	aumentarás	you will increase

Sueños y Visiones: Vocabulario de lo que tú escribiste
Dreams and Visions: Vocabulary from What You Wrote

_____

_____

_____

_____

_____

_____

_____

_____

_____

_____

_____

_____

_____

2

Gratitud

Louise Hay, la reina de las afirmaciones positivas, empezaba su día dando gracias no sólo por las cosas importantes en su vida, sino que también daba gracias por todas las cosas pequeñas que son, al fin y al cabo, de alguna manera también importantes. Daba gracias por su almohada, su cama, sus pantuflas, su desayuno, sus pijamas, su ropa, su auto...

Dar gracias por algo o el valorar alguna cosa nos ayuda a mejorar nuestro estado de ánimo. Es buena práctica no sólo en las mañanas, sino también cuando uno está de mal humor o con el ánimo bajo. Nos ayuda a transportarnos de la negatividad al optimismo y la esperanza.

Hoy yo di gracias por lo siguiente: mi marido, mi familia, mi salud, mis vecinos, el café con canela, el buen clima, mi trabajo, la electricidad y la ventana nueva en mi cocina que ahora puedo abrir, entre otras cosas.

Ejercicio

Di y anota en español por lo menos cinco cosas por las cuales hoy estás agradecido. Pueden ser cosas grandes o pequeñas; tú decides. Busca las palabras que no te sepas y agrégalas a tu glosario.

Puedes practicar este ejercicio a diario o cada tantos días, dando gracias por las mismas cosas para que así te memorices el vocabulario. Luego, después de que pase algún tiempo, haz una lista con otras cosas que agradeces tener en tu vida y practica la nueva lista unos días. De vez en cuando, asegúrate de volver a revisar las listas iniciales para mantener ese vocabulario activo.

2

Gratitude

Louise Hay, the queen of positive affirmations, began her day giving thanks not just for the important things in her life but also for all the little things that, in the end, are important in their own way. She gave thanks for her pillow, her bed, her bedroom slippers, her breakfast, her pajamas, her clothes, her car ...

Giving thanks or appreciating something helps us improve our state of mind. It's a good practice not only in the mornings but also when we're in a bad mood or in a negative state of mind. It helps transport us from negativity to optimism and hope.

Today I gave thanks for the following: my husband, my family, my health, my neighbors, coffee with cinnamon, good weather, my work, electricity, and my new kitchen window that I can now open, among other things.

Exercise

Say and write down at least five things in Spanish for which you are grateful today. They can be big or small. You decide. Look up the terms you don't know, and add them to your glossary.

You can practice this exercise daily or every few days, giving thanks for the same things so you can memorize the vocabulary. Then, after a while, write a list of different things you're grateful for in your life, and practice with the new list for several days. Make sure to go back to your initial lists from time to time to keep that vocabulary active.

Glosario: Gratitud
Glossary: Gratitude

1.	reina	queen
2.	al fin y al cabo	in the end, after all, when all is said and done
3.	almohada	pillow
4.	pantuflas	bedroom slippers
5.	estado de ánimo	state of mind, frame of mind
6.	mal humor	bad mood
7.	ánimo bajo	negative state of mind, feeling down
8.	esperanza	hope
9.	marido	husband
10.	vecinos	neighbors
11.	canela	cinnamon
12.	clima	climate
13.	entre otras cosas	among other things
14.	agradecido	grateful, thankful
15.	a diario	daily
16.	cada tantos días	every so many days
17.	de vez en cuando	from time to time
18.	asegúrate	make sure
19.	revisar	review
20.	mantener	maintain

Gratitud: Vocabulario de lo que tú escribiste
Gratitude: Vocabulary from What You Wrote

_____

_____

_____

_____

_____

_____

_____

_____

_____

_____

_____

_____

_____

3

Intenciones

Es bueno empezar el día con alguna intención – o varias. Sirve como un mapa para la trayectoria del día. Podría ser simplemente algo así como, <<Hoy disfrutaré de mi día. Actuaré como si hoy fuese un día especial, aunque sea de lo más ordinario. Trataré de ver el lado positivo de las cosas y me esforzaré por mantenerme calmado y relajado y si no siempre lo logro, tendré paciencia conmigo mismo>>.

Las intenciones se pueden formular y afirmar a cualquier hora, no sólo al comienzo del día. Es aconsejable repetirlas varias veces al día para darles más fuerza. También es buena idea declarar nuestras intenciones antes de acostarnos; pueden ser las mismas que ya repetiste durante el día o pueden ser intenciones nuevas. Por ejemplo, <<esta noche dormiré bien; tendré lindos sueños; despertaré con energía; me acordaré de mis sueños al despertar; soy hija o hijo del universo y mis problemas se solucionarán fácilmente>>.

Ejercicio

Anota una o dos intenciones en español y repítelas en el transcurso del día todas las veces que tú quieras. También puedes escribirlas en inglés y traducirlas al español. Anota el vocabulario en tu glosario. Puedes repetir las mismas intenciones durante una semana o durante varios días hasta que te aprendas bien el vocabulario y después cambiarlas por nuevas. Asegúrate de volver a repasar tu vocabulario nuevo para que no se te olvide.

3

Intentions

It's good to start the day with an intention—or several. It can serve as a map for the day's trajectory. It could be something as simple as this: "Today I will enjoy my day. I will act as if today were a special day even though it may be most ordinary. I will try to see the positive side of things and make an effort to remain calm and relaxed, and if I don't always succeed, I will be patient with myself."

Intentions can be created and stated at any time, not just at the beginning of the day. It's good to repeat them throughout the day to give them more power. It's also a good idea to state intentions before going to bed; these can be the same intentions you repeated throughout the day or new intentions. Here is an example: "Tonight I will sleep well; I will have lovely dreams; I will wake up with energy; I will remember my dreams when I awaken; I am a son or daughter of the universe, and my problems will be resolved easily."

Exercise

Write down one or two intentions in Spanish, and repeat them throughout the day as many times as you wish. You can also write them in English and translate them into Spanish. Write down your vocabulary in your glossary. You can repeat the same intentions for a week or for several days until you learn the vocabulary and then change them for new intentions. Make sure to review your new vocabulary often so you don't forget it.

Glosario: Intenciones
Glossary: Intentions

1.	simplemente	simply
2.	disfrutaré	I will enjoy
3.	actuaré	I will act
4.	si hoy fuese	if today were
5.	trataré	I will try
6.	esforzaré	I will try, I will make an effort
7.	relajado	relaxed
8.	si no siempre lo logro	if I don't always achieve it
9.	formular	formulate, create
10.	es aconsejable	it is advised, it's good advice
11.	fuerza	power, force
12.	antes de acostarnos	before we go to bed (in this context; in other contexts, it can mean to lie down)
13.	repetiste	repeated (that you repeated)
14.	despertaré	I will wake up
15.	solucionarán	will resolve
16.	fácilmente	easily
17.	en el transcurso del día	throughout the day
18.	traducirlas	translate them
19.	hasta que te aprendas	until you learn
20.	cambiarlas	change them

Intenciones: Vocabulario de lo que tú escribiste
Intentions: Vocabulary from What You Wrote

_____

_____

_____

_____

_____

_____

_____

_____

_____

_____

_____

_____

4

El día de los muertos

En México, festejar el día de los muertos tiene como propósito principal el brindar homenaje a nuestros antepasados. Es una manera no sólo de recordarlos, sino que también sirve para enseñarles a las generaciones más jóvenes acerca de cómo eran. Contamos anécdotas sobre ellos, hablamos sobre sus idiosincrasias, de las cosas que les gustaban – comidas, canciones, pasatiempos, etc.- para que la nueva generación conozca a los parientes que ya pasaron a otro mundo.

Ejercicio

Anota los nombres de al menos tres personas ya fallecidas. No tienen que ser parientes tuyos; pueden ser simplemente personas que tú admirabas. Haz una lista en español de algunas cualidades que ellos hayan tenido. Como ejemplo, comparto aquí una lista de personas que yo admiraba junto con algunos detalles de sus vidas:

Mi mamá: Amante de la vida y generosa; le encantaba la comida típica mexicana, especialmente la de Sonora y nunca se cansaba de oír la música de los mariachis.

Mi papá: Gran motivador; fumaba pipa y se podía pasar la noche entera leyendo.

Mi tía Yeyé: Tenía una paciencia tremenda; era una mujer sabia de buen juicio.

Mi hermano Erik: Era excelente jugador de ajedrez, inteligente, lleno de curiosidad y amigo fiel. Le encantaba la astronomía.

Mi primo David: Tenía un sentido del humor increíble y una pasión para aprender cosas nuevas. Su pasatiempo era comprar y vender libros.

Variando el ejercicio

Otra manera de hacer este ejercicio es de seleccionar personas que aún viven, en vez de seleccionar a personas fallecidas. Anota el nombre de varias personas que conozcas o admires y escribe las cualidades que poseen y detalles sobre sus vidas, en español.

4

The Day of the Dead

Paying homage to our ancestors is a main objective of the Mexican Day of the Dead celebration. It's a way not only to remember them but also to teach the younger generations what their ancestors were like. We tell stories about them, and we talk about their idiosyncrasies, including the things they liked (food, songs, pastimes, etc.) so that the newer generation can get to know relatives who have crossed to another world.

Exercise

Write down the names of at least three deceased persons. They don't have to be related to you; they could simply be people you admired. Write a list in Spanish of some qualities they had. As an example, the following is a list of people I admired along with some details about their lives.

- My mom, lover of life and generous. She loved traditional Mexican food, especially food from Sonora, and she never tired of listening to mariachi music.

- My dad, a great motivator. He smoked a pipe and could spend the entire night reading.

- My aunt Yeyé, who had tremendous patience. She was a wise woman with great judgment.

- My brother Erik, who was an excellent chess player. He was intelligent, full of curiosity, and a loyal friend. He loved astronomy.

- My cousin David, who had an amazing sense of humor and a passion for learning new things. His hobby was to buy and sell books.

Varying the Exercise

An alternative is to do the same exercise but instead of choosing people who are already deceased choosing people who are still alive. Write down the names of several people you know or admire, and then write in Spanish qualities they possess and details about their lives.

Glosario: Día de los muertos
Glossary: Day of the Dead

1.	festejar	celebrate
2.	brindar homenaje	pay homage *(brindar has different meanings in different contexts; I encourage you to explore this word)*
3.	antepasados	ancestors
4.	manera	means, a way, ways to
5.	recordarlos	remember them
6.	más jóvenes	younger
7.	contamos	we tell
8.	les gustaban	they liked
9.	canciones	songs
10.	pasatiempos	hobbies, pastimes
11.	parientes	relatives
12.	mundo	world
13.	fallecidas	deceased
14.	admirabas	you admired
15.	cualidades	qualities
16.	comida típica	traditional food
17.	fumaba pipa	smoked a pipe
18.	ajedrez	chess
19.	amigo fiel	loyal friend
20.	sentido del humor	sense of humor

Día de los muertos: Vocabulario de lo que tú escribiste
Day of the dead: Vocabulary from What You Wrote

_____

_____

_____

_____

_____

_____

_____

_____

_____

_____

_____

_____

_____

5

Canciones

Ejercicio

Piensa en una canción que te emocione; que te haga sonreír. Todos tenemos una canción que, al oírla, nos llenamos de emociones positivas. Piensa en esa canción. Puede ser que tengas varias. Si no tienes, pues busca una. No tiene que tener letra inspiradora – sólo tiene que motivarte o subirte el ánimo. Busca la letra de tu canción. Si está en inglés, busca su traducción al español o tradúcela tú mismo – cuando menos el coro o algunos versos que te gusten. Escúchala a menudo; te inspirará y reforzará el vocabulario de tu segundo idioma. Pega la letra de la canción en la puerta del refrigerador, en un tablero de corcho, o llévala en tu billetera o bolsillo. Puedes hacer lo mismo con diferentes versos o diferentes canciones – una canción a la semana o una al mes, como tú prefieras; pero que sea lo suficiente para que te motive y aprendas el vocabulario. Estas son algunas de mis favoritas.

- "La vida es un carnaval" de Celia Cruz

- "Correteando un sueño" ("Runnin' Down a Dream") de Tom Petty

- "Vivir mi vida" de Marc Anthony

- "Yo canto" de Laura Pausini

- "Hoy es domingo" de Diego Torres y Rubén Blades

- "Bonito" de Jarabe de Palo

- "Sigo de pie" ("I'm Still Standing") de Elton John

- "Feliz" ("Happy") de Pharrell Williams

5

Songs

Exercise

Think of a song that moves you and makes you smile. We all have a song that fills us with positive emotions when we listen to it. Think about that song. Maybe you have several. If you don't have one, then look for one. It doesn't have to have inspiring lyrics; it just needs to motivate you or lift you up. Find the lyrics of your song. If it's in English, look for its Spanish translation or translate it yourself—even if it's just the chorus or a few verses that you like. Listen to it often; it will inspire you and reinforce the vocabulary of your second language. Put the lyrics on the refrigerator, on a bulletin board, or in your wallet or in your pocket. You can do this with different verses or different songs—one song per week or per month, however you wish. Just enough so that it will motivate you and you can learn the vocabulary. These are some of my favorites:

- "Life Is a Carnival" ("La vida es un carnaval") by Celia Cruz

- "Running Down a Dream" ("Correteando un sueño") by Tom Petty

- "Living My Life" ("Vivir mi vida") by Marc Anthony

- "I Sing" ("Yo canto") by Laura Pausini

- "Today Is Sunday" ("Hoy es domingo") by Diego Torres and Ruben Blades

- "Nice" ("Bonito") by Jarabe de Palo

- "I'm Still Standing" ("Sigo de pie") by Elton John

- "Happy" ("Feliz") by Pharrell Williams

Glosario: Canciones
Glossary: Songs

1.	te emocione	that moves you, excites you, thrills you
2.	sonreír	to smile
3.	al oírla	upon hearing it, when one hears it
4.	emociones positivas	positive emotions
5.	varias	several
6.	inspiradora	inspiring
7.	motivarte	motivate you
8.	subirte el ánimo	lift you up, make you feel better, lift your mood
9.	la letra (de una canción)	lyrics
10.	coro (también se le dice estribillo)	chorus
11.	versos	verses
12.	escúchala	listen to it
13.	a menudo	often
14.	reforzará	it will reinforce
15.	segundo idioma	second language
16.	pega	post, stick on, paste (in this context)
17.	tablero de corcho	bulletin board
18.	billetera	wallet
19.	bolsillo	pocket
20.	correteando	chasing, running after something

Canciones: Vocabulario de lo que tú escribiste
Songs: Vocabulary from What You Wrote

_____

_____

_____

_____

_____

_____

_____

_____

_____

_____

_____

_____

6

El reino animal

A los seres humanos nos encanta atribuirles cualidades humanas a los animales. Las fábulas y los cuentos mitológicos están llenos de tales ejemplos, como la hormiguita trabajadora o la elegante y astuta pantera. Al elefante muchos le atribuyen las cualidades de la perseverancia y la paciencia; al león, la valentía; al búho, la sabiduría. Un ejemplo, en mi caso, es el correcaminos; para mí, representa el ser audaz, seguro de sí mismo y a la vez estar alegre y despreocupado, y por tal, lo considero presagio de buena suerte. También admiro al cuervo, por su fama de inteligente y misterioso y porque en los cuentos tiende a ser asociado como mensajero del porvenir. Las mariposas me inspiran libertad y alegría.

Ejercicio

Piensa en un animal que para que ti simbolice ciertos atributos que tú respetas, quisieras adquirir o desarrollar. Escribe en español el nombre del animal junto con las cualidades que le atribuyes. De tanto en tanto regresa a este ejercicio y piensa en otros animales. Dependiendo de lo que esté pasando en tu vida o de tu estado de ánimo, pensarás en diferentes animales y cualidades. No se te olvide anotar los términos que te surjan durante este ejercicio en tu glosario.

6

The Animal Kingdom

Humans love to attribute human qualities to animals. Fables and mythological stories are filled with examples of this, from the hardworking ant to the elegant and astute panther. Many people attribute the qualities of perseverance and patience to elephants, bravery to the lion, and wisdom to the owl. In my case, for example, roadrunners represent being daring, self-confident, happy, and carefree all at the same time, which is why I consider them an omen of good fortune. I also admire the crow, who is famous for being intelligent and because in stories the crow tends to be associated with mystery and as a messenger of what's to come. Butterflies to me inspire freedom and joy.

Exercise

Think about an animal that to you symbolizes qualities that you respect, would like to acquire, or would like to develop more fully. Write the name of the animal in Spanish along with the qualities you attribute to it. Return to this exercise from time to time, thinking about other animals. Depending on what's going on in your life or your mood, you'll think of different animals and attributes. Don't forget to write the terms in your glossary that come up during this exercise.

Glosario: El reino animal
Glossary: The Animal Kingdom

1.	seres humanos	human beings
2.	fábulas	fables
3.	mitológicos	mythological
4.	hormiguita	little ant
5.	atribuyen	they attribute
6.	valentía	bravery
7.	búho	owl
8.	sabiduría	wisdom
9.	correcaminos	roadrunner
10.	audaz	daring
11.	seguro de sí mismo	sure of itself, self-confident
12.	despreocupado	worry free, carefree
13.	por tal	as such, which is why, because of that (in this context)
14.	presagio	sign, omen
15.	cuervo	crow
16.	cuentos	stories
17.	mensajero	messenger
18.	porvenir	future, things to come
19.	mariposa	butterfly
20.	surjan	come up, arise, emerge

El reino animal: Vocabulario de lo que tú escribiste
The Animal Kingdom: Vocabulary from What You Wrote

_____

_____

_____

_____

_____

_____

_____

_____

_____

_____

_____

_____

7

Momentos especiales

Es bueno revivir los momentos felices especialmente cuando uno se siente algo cabizbajo. De hecho, es bueno hacerlo en cualquier momento. Sirve para levantarnos el ánimo y ayuda para recalibrar nuestra actitud y enfrentar los retos del día.

Ejercicio

Piensa en un momento especial en tu vida. Puede ser una ocasión importante en tu vida, como una boda o el nacimiento de algún bebé o simplemente un día o un momento lindo en cual te sentiste feliz, tranquilo, entusiasmado, alegre o algo por estilo. Por ejemplo, piensa en lo que sentías al caminar por el bosque o la playa; o lo que sentías cuando le ayudabas a tu abuela en la cocina de niño, o sencillamente lo que sientes cuando estás en tu sillón favorito. Cierra los ojos, si eso te ayuda, respira profundo y trata de sentir las emociones que experimentaste en esa ocasión. Revívelo si puedes. Describe en español, lo mejor que puedas, el evento, ocasión o momento especial. Luego, anota, en español, las emociones que sentiste. O si prefieres, escríbelo todo en inglés y luego tradúcelo al español. Vuelve a este ejercicio de vez en cuando y piensa en un evento distinto o en emociones distintas. No se te olvide repasar el vocabulario frecuentemente para reforzarlo.

7

Special Moments

It is good to relive happy moments, especially when one is feeling downcast. In fact, it's a good thing to do at any time. It helps to raise our spirits and helps to recalibrate our attitude and face the challenges of the day.

Exercise

Think of a special moment in your life. It could be an important occasion like a wedding or the birth of a baby or simply a day or a lovely moment when you felt happy, calm, excited, joyful, or something to that effect. For example, you can think about what you felt when you walked through a forest or along a beach, what you felt when you helped your grandma in the kitchen as a child, or simply what you feel when you're in your favorite easy chair. Close your eyes, if that helps, breathe deeply, and try to feel the emotions you felt on that occasion. Relive it if you can. Describe the event, moment, or special occasion in Spanish as best as you can. Then write down the feelings you felt—also in Spanish. Or if you want, write it all in English and then translate it into Spanish. Come back to this exercise from time to time and think of a different event or different feelings. Don't forget to review your vocabulary frequently to reinforce it.

Glosario: Momentos especiales
Glossary: Special Moments

1.	revivir	relive
2.	cabizbajo	downcast, crestfallen
3.	de hecho	in fact
4.	levantar el ánimo	raise spirits, lighten up a mood
5.	recalibrar	recalibrate
6.	retos	challenges
7.	boda	wedding
8.	nacimiento	birth
9.	bebé	baby
10.	feliz	happy
11.	tranquilo	calm
12.	entusiasmado	excited, enthused
13.	alegre	joyful, merry, cheerful, lively
14.	algo por el estilo	something like that, something to that effect
15.	bosque	forest
16.	playa	beach
17.	abuela	grandmother
18.	sillón	easy chair
19.	respira profundo	breathe deeply
20.	que experimentaste	that you experienced

Momentos especiales: Vocabulario de lo que tú escribiste
Special Moments: Vocabulary from What You Wrote

_____

_____

_____

_____

_____

_____

_____

_____

_____

_____

_____

_____

_____

8

Baños de naturaleza

El *Shinrin-yoku* es una terapia japonesa que ha demostrado ser beneficiosa para la salud física y mental. Se traduce como "baño forestal" o "baño de bosque" y consiste en caminar por un bosque de manera meditativa para absorber la naturaleza con todos los sentidos; fijándonos en lo que vemos, respirando profundamente, examinando cómo se siente la textura de la corteza de los arboles y de las hojas al tocarlas; sintiendo el aire en la piel; escuchando el sonido del viento y los cantos de los pájaros y recordando que formamos parte de la naturaleza.

Ejercicio

Lo ideal sería ir a un ambiente natural, convivir con la naturaleza y tomar un baño forestal. Luego, al regresar, describir en voz alta o por escrito lo que viste, oíste y sentiste. Si eso no es factible, busca un lugar en dónde no te puedan molestar y cierra los ojos. Respira profundo unas cuantas veces e imagínate que estás en un lugar bello de la naturaleza. Puede ser un lago, un bosque, el mar, el desierto sonorense; cualquier lugar que te inspire o traiga sensaciones de bienestar, paz, seguridad o alegría. Podría hasta ser un lugar mágico de colores y luces vibrantes con mariposas azules, libélulas fosforescentes, unicornios, dragones mansos, cascadas anaranjadas, lo que tú quieras. Disfruta esas sensaciones por varios minutos. Cuando abras los ojos, describe en detalle el lugar donde te imaginaste estar. Trata de hacerlo en español o si quieres, en inglés y luego lo traduces al español. Puedes también escribir lo que sentiste. Anota las palabras nuevas en tu glosario. Usa adjetivos y adverbios para ampliar tu vocabulario y recalcar las sensaciones que experimentaste. Repite este ejercicio y ve cambiando el escenario para aumentar tu vocabulario. La idea es que aumentes tu vocabulario en cuanto a terminología relativa a la naturaleza; que vayas adquiriendo términos como, por ejemplo, río, rocas, roble, playa, arena, pez estrella, etc. Y a la vez, experimentar un baño forestal ya sea real o imaginado.

8

Nature Baths

Shinrin-yoku is a Japanese therapy that has shown to be beneficial for physical and mental health. It's translated as "forest bathing," and it consists of walking through a forest in a meditative manner, absorbing nature with all your senses, paying attention to what you see, breathing deeply, feeling the texture of the tree bark and the leaves when you touch them, feeling the air on your skin, listening to the sound of the wind and the birdsongs, and remembering that we are part of nature.

Exercise

The ideal would be for you to go to a natural environment, commune with nature, and take a forest bath. Then when you come back, describe out loud and/or in writing what you saw, heard, and felt. If that's not feasible, find a place where you won't be bothered, close your eyes, breathe deeply a few times, and imagine that you're in a beautiful place in nature. It can be a lake, a forest, the sea, the Sonoran Desert, or any place that inspires you or brings you feelings of well-being, peace, safety, or joy. It could even be a magical place with vibrant colors and lights, blue butterflies, phosphorescent dragonflies, unicorns, tame dragons, orange waterfalls—whatever you want. Enjoy those sensations for a few minutes. When you open your eyes, describe in detail the place. Try to do it in Spanish, or write it in

English and then translate it into Spanish. You can also describe what you felt. Write down any new words in your glossary. Use adjectives and adverbs to extend your vocabulary and reinforce the feelings you experienced. Repeat this exercise, and change the scene so you can expand your vocabulary. The idea is for you to increase your vocabulary in relation to nature; to acquire terms of nature (river, rocks, oak tree, beach, sand, starfish, etc.), and experience a forest bath, be it real or imagined.

Glosario: Baños de naturaleza
Glossary: Nature Baths

1.	terapia	therapy
2.	sentidos	senses
3.	corteza de los arboles	tree bark
4.	ambiente natural	natural environment
5.	factible	feasible
6.	molestar	bother
7.	desierto sonorense	Sonoran Desert
8.	bienestar	well-being
9.	seguridad	safety
10.	luces	lights
11.	vibrantes	vibrant
12.	libélulas	dragonflies
13.	fosforescente	phosphorescent
14.	mansos	tame
15.	cascadas	waterfalls
16.	anaranjada	orange (as a feminine adjective)
17.	escenario	scene
18.	roble	oak tree
19.	arena	sand
20.	pez estrella	starfish

Baños de naturaleza: Vocabulario de lo que tú escribiste
Nature Baths: Vocabulary from What You Wrote

_____

_____

_____

_____

_____

_____

_____

_____

_____

_____

_____

_____

_____

9

Comida reconfortante

La comida no sólo nos sostiene y nutre; también nos ayuda a disfrutar el momento y a festejar eventos y encuentros especiales, ya sean bodas, días festivos o tertulias. Hoy en día se habla de la "comida reconfortante" para referirnos a aquello que comemos cuando nuestro estado de ánimo está bajo y queremos sentirnos mejor. A veces, los aromas de ciertas comidas son suficiente para desencadenar emociones y recuerdos muy antiguos. El propósito de este ejercicio es el de revivir sensaciones gratas, practicar describirlas en español y explorar la terminología culinaria en los dos idiomas.

Ejercicio:

Hay tres opciones para el siguiente ejercicio.

- Opción 1: Recuerda un evento agradable en tu vida en el cual hubo comida. Toma unos minutos para recordar el evento y revivir las sensaciones placenteras. Luego, piensa en la comida y las bebidas que se consumieron en esa ocasión. Descríbelas en voz alta o por escrito preferiblemente en español, pero si quieres, puedes escribirlas en inglés y traducirlas luego al español.

- Opción 2: Describe con detalle lo que tú consideres como "comida reconfortante." Por ejemplo, para mí serían: el helado de chocolate con almendras, el mole veracruzano, una tortilla de maíz recién hecha y las calabacitas con queso y mantequilla como las hacía mi mamá cuando yo era chiquita.

- Opción 3: Describe en español la comida típica de algún día festivo; por ejemplo, lo que se come en el Día de Acción de Gracias o el Cuatro de Julio. Habla en detalle de los ingredientes y los sabores (por ejemplo, agrio, dulce, salado, amargo). Si quieres, escribe las recetas de los platillos en español anotando, como siempre, el vocabulario que vayas aprendiendo. Hasta puedes hablar de los utensilios que se usan para cocinar los platos.

Recomiendo que veas videos de cocina en español, como los del *Gipsy Chef* y *Cocina con Rosa* para ampliar tu vocabulario culinario.

9

Comfort Food

Food doesn't just sustain and nourish us; it also helps us enjoy the moment and celebrate special events and encounters, be they weddings, holidays, or social gatherings. Nowadays we speak of "comfort food," which is what you eat when you're in a negative state of mind and want to feel better. Sometimes the smell of certain foods is enough to trigger very old emotions and memories. The purpose of this exercise is to relive pleasant feelings, practice describing them in Spanish, and explore culinary terminology in both languages.

Exercise

There are three options for the following exercise:

- Option 1: Recall a pleasant event in your life when there was food. Take a few minutes to relive the feelings of enjoyment. Then think of the food and beverages that were consumed on that occasion. Describe them out loud or in writing in Spanish, or you can write them in English and then translate them into Spanish.

- Option 2: Describe in detail what you consider to be comfort food. For example, for me it would be chocolate ice cream with almonds, *mole* from Veracruz, a freshly made corn tortilla, and zucchini with butter and cheese the way my mother made it when I was little.

- <u>Option 3:</u> Describe in Spanish the traditional food for a given holiday, such as what you eat during Thanksgiving or the Fourth of July. Speak in detail about the ingredients and the flavors (e.g., sour, sweet, salty, or bitter). If you want, write down the recipes for the dishes in Spanish while keeping track, as always, of the vocabulary that you are learning. You may even talk about the utensils needed to cook the dishes.

I recommend you watch cooking videos in Spanish, such as *Gipsy Chef* and *Cocina con Rosa*, to improve your culinary vocabulary.

Glosario: Comida reconfortante
Glossary: Comfort Food

1.	nutre	nourish
2.	disfrutar el momento	enjoy the moment
3.	bodas	weddings
4.	tertulia	social gathering (usually with a small group of friends involving lively discussions)
5.	hoy en día	nowadays
6.	estado de ánimo bajo	bad mood, negative state of mind
7.	desencadenar	trigger
8.	gratas	pleasing, agreeable, pleasant
9.	placenteras	pleasant, enjoyable
10.	helado de chocolate	chocolate ice cream
11.	almendras	almonds
12.	recién hecha	freshly made
13.	calabacitas	zucchini (in Mexican Spanish)
14.	mantequilla	butter
15.	días festivos	holidays
16.	Día de Acción de Gracias	Thanksgiving Day
17.	agrio	sour
18.	dulce	sweet
19.	salado	salty
20.	amargo	bitter

Comida reconfortante: Vocabulario de lo que tú escribiste
Comfort Food: Vocabulary from What You Wrote

_____

_____

_____

_____

_____

_____

_____

_____

_____

_____

_____

_____

_____

_____

_____

10

Palabras inspiradoras

El siguiente ejercicio meditativo tiene que ver con frases inspiradoras. Existen frases que nos inspiran cada vez que las oímos o leemos. Estas palabras inspiradoras o motivantes pueden provenir de autores, personas célebres o gente que de alguna manera nos ha influido. Este ejercicio tiene como propósito ponerte en un estado de ánimo positivo al leer o recitar citas inspiradoras, así como también aprender a decirlas en español. Puedes buscar por internet frases dichas originalmente en español o las traducciones de citas de autores o personajes que te gusten. Claro, siempre tienes la opción de traducirlas tú mismo. La traducción ayuda mucho con la adquisición de vocabulario por la cantidad de investigación que requiere.

Aquí están unas de mis frases favoritas. Puedes usar estas o buscar otras. Es bueno repasarlas constantemente para que retengas el vocabulario.

1. "No preguntes qué necesita el mundo. Pregúntate qué es lo que te hace sentir vivo y has eso. Porque lo que el mundo necesita es gente que se sienta viva." – Howard Thurman

2. "La preocupación es como una silla mecedora; te da algo que hacer, pero nunca te lleva a ninguna parte." – Erma Bombeck

3. "Si te caes siete veces, levántate ocho." – Proverbio japonés

4. "Regálate cinco minutos de contemplación y asómbrate de todo lo que veas a tu alrededor. Sal y dirige tu atención a los muchos milagros que te rodean. Este régimen de cinco minutos diarios de reconocimiento y gratitud te ayudara a vivir la vida con fascinación." – Wayne Dyer

5. "Si puedes verte como un artista y puedes ver que tu vida es tu propia creación, entonces ¿por qué no crear para ti mismo la historia más bella? La vida es sólo un sueño y si creas tu vida con amor, tu sueño se convertirá en una obra maestra." – Miguel Ruiz

6. "La palabra es la herramienta más poderosa que tiene el ser humano; es un instrumento mágico. Pero las palabras también son como una espada de doble filo: pueden crear el sueño más bello o destruir todo lo que te rodea." – Miguel Ruiz

7. "Nuestro temor más profundo no es el ser inadecuado. Nuestro temor más profundo es el de tener un poder inconmensurable. Es nuestra luz, no nuestra oscuridad lo que nos asusta. Nos preguntamos, <<¿quién soy yo para ser brillante, precioso, talentoso, fabuloso?>> Mas bien la pregunta que debes hacerte es: ¿quién eres tú para

no serlo? Eres hija o hijo de Dios. El jugar a ser pequeño no le sirve al mundo. No tiene nada de iluminador el encogerse para que las personas que te rodean no se sientan inseguras. Nuestro destino es brillar, así como lo hacen los niños. Nacemos para manifestar la gloria de Dios que está en nuestro interior. No sólo en el interior de algunos; está en todos nosotros. Al permitir que brille nuestra luz, inconscientemente le damos permiso a otros para hacer lo mismo. Al librarnos de nuestro miedo, nuestra presencia automáticamente liberará a otros." – Marianne Williamson

8. "Tienes una sabiduría dentro de ti – escúchala. Tienes una luz interior – siente como brilla. Tienes el poder de hablar, de actuar y de manifestar cosas en el mundo – deja que tu sabiduría y tu luz te guíen al hacerlo." –Michael Neill

10

Inspirational Words

The following meditative exercise has to do with inspirational quotes. There are quotes that inspire us every time we hear or read them. These inspiring or motivating words can come from writers, famous people, or persons who have influenced you in one way or another. The purpose of this exercise is to put you in a positive state of mind by reading or reciting inspiring quotes while learning to say them in Spanish. You can find original Spanish quotes on the internet or look for Spanish translations of quotes from authors or celebrities you like. Of course, you always have the option of translating them yourself. Translating greatly helps with the acquisition of vocabulary due to the research it requires.

Below are some of my favorite inspirational quotes. You can use these or look for others. It's good to review them constantly so you can retain the vocabulary.

1. Don't ask what the world needs. Ask what makes you come alive and go do it. Because what the world needs is people who have come alive. (Howard Thurman)

2. Worry is like a rocking chair: it gives you something to do but never gets you anywhere. (Erma Bombeck)

3. If you fall down seven times, get up eight. (Japanese proverb)

4. Give yourself a gift of five minutes of contemplation in awe of everything you see around you. Go outside and turn your attention to the many miracles around you. This five-minutes-a-day regimen of appreciation and gratitude will help you to focus your life in awe. (Wayne Dyer)

5. If you can see yourself as an artist, and you can see that your life is your own creation, then why not create the most beautiful story for yourself? Life is nothing but a dream and if you create your life with love, your dream becomes a masterpiece of art. (Miguel Ruiz)

6. Words are the most powerful tools you have as a human being; they are instruments of magic. But they are like a double-edged sword: they can create the most beautiful dream or destroy everything around you. (Miguel Ruiz)

7. Our deepest fear is not that we are inadequate. Our deepest fear is that we are powerful beyond measure. It is our light, not our darkness that most frightens us. We ask ourselves, "Who am I to be brilliant, gorgeous, talented, fabulous?" Actually, who are you not to be? You are a child of God. Your playing small does not serve the world. There is nothing enlightened about shrinking so that other people won't feel insecure around you. We are all meant to shine, as children do. We were born to make manifest the glory of God that

is within us. It's not just in some of us; it's in everyone. And as we let our own light shine, we unconsciously give other people permission to do the same. As we are liberated from our own fear, our presence automatically liberates others. (Marianne Williamson)

8. You have a wisdom inside you—listen for it. You have a light inside you—feel its glow. You have the power to speak and act and make things manifest in the world—let your wisdom and light guide you as you do. (Michael Neill)

Glosario: Palabras inspiradoras
Glossary: Inspirational Words

1.	frases inspiradoras (también se usa "citas")	inspiring quotes
2.	autores	authors
3.	personas célebres	famous people
4.	preocupación	worry
5.	silla mecedora	rocking chair
6.	regálate	give yourself a gift
7.	asómbrate	be in awe
8.	creación	creation
9.	obra maestra	masterpiece
10.	herramienta	tool
11.	espada	sword
12.	doble filo	double-edged
13.	destruir	destroy
14.	lo que te rodea	what surrounds you
15.	temor	fear
16.	inconmensurable	immeasurable
17.	oscuridad	darkness
18.	talentoso	talented
19.	encogerse	shrink, make oneself small
20.	inconscientemente	unconsciously

Palabras inspiradoras: Vocabulario de lo que tú escribiste.
Inspiring Words: Vocabulary from What You Wrote.

_____

_____

_____

_____

_____

_____

_____

_____

_____

_____

_____

_____

_____

I hope you have enjoyed this book and that it has inspired you in your journey as a bilingual meditator. I would love to hear your comments. You can connect with me through my website, TheConfidentInterpreter.com or via Facebook. If you're intcrested in listening to free audio recordings of Chapters 1 & 2, send me an email at TheConfidentInterpreter@gmail.com.

¡Saludos!

Yvette

Printed in the United States
By Bookmasters